Philippians
At His Feet Studies

By Hope A. Blanton and Christine B. Gordon

Revised Edition

Philippians

Contents

How to Use This Study

There is no right way to lead a Bible study. Every Bible study group is made up of different types of people with various needs and dynamics. These are some suggestions that might be helpful when using At His Feet Studies. Read it through. Use what you want. Forget the rest. We're glad you're here.

A different approach to a familiar method

As with many Bible studies you're familiar with, we follow a pattern of observation, interpretation, and application, but the presentation may be a little different than what you're used to. Instead of bouncing between those three tasks, we group them.

First, you will read a biblical passage, and using the Observation Questions, you'll note the people mentioned, terms used, commands given, actions taken, and so on. This is arguably the most important step, as the Word of God itself is powerful and active.

In the next section, you will interpret the biblical passage with help from seminary-trained Chris. The Interpretation section is written in the style of most commentaries, offering a verse-by-verse explanation of the biblical passage. This section is rooted in study of the original language and multiple sources, including commentaries, original language helps, sermons, theological treatises, and personal conversations with seminary professors.

Finally, you will apply the biblical text to your life, assisted by licensed therapist Hope and her heart-engaging Reflection Questions.

In this way, you will read, interpret, and then reflect on a larger passage as a whole, keeping the words and message in their context.

What do I do each day?

You can read through and complete the entire study in one sitting or break it up. If you'd like to spread out your preparation a bit more, break it into three days: On day 1, read the biblical passage and complete the Observation Questions. On day 2, read the Interpretation section. On day 3, complete the Reflection Questions. You could even add a day 4 and attempt to memorize or simply meditate on the focus verse and/or write down your thoughts in the space for "Reflections, curiosities, frustrations."

How do I lead a group through this study?

It is always a good idea to read through the biblical passage out loud at the beginning of your time together. After reading the Scripture aloud, choose one or two Observation Questions and answer them as a group.

If most of your group has had a chance to read the Interpretation section on their own, ask them what stood out to them in that section and talk through parts of the commentary they may have highlighted. If you are leading a group with participants who have not had the time to read through the Interpretation section on their own, take the time to read it out loud as a group before asking this question.

Next, choose three or four of your favorite Reflection Questions and allow time for everyone who would like to offer their answers. These questions are written with the aim of both engaging your own heart and also engaging one another's hearts as you study together.

If you have the time, do all of the above *and* walk through all of the Reflection Questions. If you'd like, you could ask the group what questions or frustrations arose during their study.

Want an extra challenge?

Issue the challenge to your group to memorize the focus verse and say it together when you reconvene.

Questions? Reach out!

We would love to hear from you. Write us at athisfeetstudies@gmail.com.

Introduction

The History Behind the Pages of Philippians

For an overview of the historical context of Paul's letter to the Philippians, read Acts 16.

As is often the case, God began the church at Philippi using unexpected means—closed doors and a stint in prison. Twice in Acts 16, we are told that the Holy Spirit did not allow Paul and Timothy to go through with their plans to preach the gospel in Asia. They must have asked, waited, found one closed door to Asia, asked, waited, and been turned away again in Bithynia.

Finally the Lord opened a door, speaking to Paul in the night with the vision of a man in the region of Macedonia asking for help. Paul and his companions responded, taking a boat through the Aegean Sea, reaching land in Neapolis, and finally ending up in Philippi, about ten miles inland. The closed doors in Asia led these missionaries to the Philippians, where God had already been at work.

The city of Philippi was named for Philip II, king of Macedonia in 356 B.C. By the first century A.D., Philippi was partially populated by Roman war veterans. These soldiers had been given land that was stolen from native Philippians by Augustus, later to be Rome's first emperor. Philippi became an important trade city because it was on the Via Egnatia, which at the time was *the* major road of the Roman Empire. The city Paul walked into during his first visit in 49 A.D. would have been a busy political center, populated by somewhere between ten and fifteen thousand Greeks and Romans.

God had been working ahead of Paul and his friends in the hearts of a group of women in Philippi, drawing them to the God of Israel. When Paul and his companions arrived in the town, they did not find a synagogue, which required ten Jewish men. However, on the Sabbath, they went to the river, which was where they would have expected to find a group of God-fearers if one existed in the city. There they found both Jewish women and Greek women who were already practicing some of the Jewish religion. Among these women was Lydia, probably a wealthy merchant, who was soon converted and baptized. She opened her home to Paul and the others, and it served as a focal point for the growth of the church in the city.

While in Philippi, Paul exorcized a demon from a slave girl and therefore stopped her fortune-telling powers. This angered the girl's owners because it cut off their source of income, and so Paul and Silas landed in jail after a heavy beating. This must have greatly discouraged and even confused the baby church at Philippi. But when God sent an earthquake and opened both the doors of the prison and the chains of the prisoners, the jailer who was in charge of them was converted. The jailer and his entire household were baptized, and the Philippian church continued to grow.

Fast forward ten years. Apparently, the Philippians, though not a wealthy church as a whole, had sent several financial gifts to Paul since his visit. They had probably also sent multiple letters, and by the time Paul wrote this letter, they had had a relationship of mutual ministry and encouragement for years. Paul was probably under house arrest in Rome awaiting trial. The Philippians knew this and were concerned for him. They sent Epaphroditus, one of their own members, with another gift to encourage Paul. But Epaphroditus became ill. Paul sent him back to relieve their anxiety and pass a letter back to them. He planned to send Timothy and then hoped to visit them himself.

So what did Paul need this beloved church to know? What precious subject did he broach in a letter to be delivered by hand, requiring days of dangerous and expensive travel? Paul sent the letter with Epaphroditus to thank the Philippians for their gift. He also wrote to reframe for them his imprisonment. He had suffered, for sure, and they would have remembered Paul's time in prison while in their own city. But Paul wanted to encourage them by telling them the good that had happened because of his chains. He wanted them, and subsequently us, to use him as an example of how to live as believers while suffering through hardships, persecutions, and trials.

But Paul wrote for another reason: to confront the disunity of the Philippian church. Paul specifically named two women whom he respected as coworkers and who struggled to agree or just get along. Notice that Paul did not write off these women or dismiss them. He dignified them as leaders and confronted them head on as fellow ambassadors for Christ. They mattered to him. Their actions mattered. Their attitudes also mattered.

Paul's words, directives, and encouragement are just as pertinent to believers in the twenty-first century as they were to those in the first century. May we hear what the Spirit says to his church, and may God grant us the will to be, as Paul wrote in Philippians 2, "of the same mind, having the same love, being in full accord and of one mind."

Study 1

To All the Saints

Read Philippians 1:1–11

Observation Questions

1. What was Paul thanking the Philippians for?

2. Why did Paul feel so strongly about the Philippians?

3. What was Paul's prayer for the Philippians?

Interpretation

Philippians 1:1–2. The greetings in letters in Paul's day almost always followed a particular form: sender, receiver, and a wish for good health. Here we see Paul using the same form but in a way that has been transformed by Christ. First, Paul named the senders. Paul wrote along with his co-sender, Timothy, the son of a believing Jewish mother and a Greek father. Paul had circumcised Timothy for the purpose of evangelism among the Jews. Timothy was probably the one physically writing the letter as Paul dictated.

What was Paul's title for himself and Timothy? Executive pastors? Directors of evangelism? Nope. Servants of Jesus Christ. The word "servants" here is better translated as "slaves," a term that would have been familiar to first-century people since a large chunk of the population of Philippi at the time were slaves. Some people were born into slavery, and some actually sold themselves into servitude to pay off a debt. Conditions for slaves were varied, from comfortable to wretched. Paul believed himself to be a slave to his Lord, the personal property of Jesus Christ. If Paul had had an office, the nameplate on the door would have read, "Slave of Jesus."

Next, Paul named the recipients of the letter. Notice that Paul did not address "the Philippian church" or "my Christian friends at Philippi" or even "my brothers and sisters." He addressed them as the saints in Christ Jesus. This was their distinguishing attribute, their just classification. Before all else, they were saints in Christ. Unlike our twenty-first-century interpretations of the word *saint,* which include things like exceptional holiness or a life of sacrifice, Paul would have meant for these people to understand themselves as the Old Testament people of God were designated: holy ones, set apart ones. As Karl Barth writes, "Holy people are unholy people who nevertheless as such have been singled out, claimed, and requisitioned by God for his control for his use for himself who is holy."[1]

The phrase "in Christ Jesus" refers to the Philippians' union with Christ, their unbreakable connection with him. Paul essentially addressed these dear brothers and sisters by saying, "To you, the men and women who have been chosen and claimed by God for his holy work, who are unshakably connected to Jesus…" Is this the way you define yourself? Is this your first thought when someone asks you who you are? Unlike the voices in our heads who accuse, God names us this way, as the ones he picked and tethered to Jesus.

Finally, Paul replaces a wish for good health with greetings of grace and peace. This is how God approaches his chosen people, with grace and peace. As Gordon Fee writes, "The sum total of God's activity toward his human creatures is found in the word 'grace.' … Nothing is deserved, nothing can be achieved."[2]

Philippians 1:3–6. Paul described his experience of praying for the Philippians as one of joy. Why? It couldn't have been because of his circumstances—he was in prison. In fact, Christian joy has nothing to do with our present situation but transcends all difficulties and discomforts. The source of our joy is the promise that Jesus Christ is the same yesterday, today, and tomorrow. Our joy originates in the confidence that all of Jesus's promises of presence and relationship are trustworthy.

Paul used the word "partnership" in verse 5 the way we would talk about a trade union or some other group that exists for the benefit of its members. He considered the church in Philippi to be his collaborators, his teammates. And the fruit of transformed lives that he had seen in them over the past ten years made him confident that it had been God working in them. God had worked salvation in them and would continue to sanctify them until the day of Christ Jesus, the day when Jesus will return again to judge the living and the dead.

Our hope for sanctification is the same today as it was for the Philippians then. God wooed us, began his work in us by his Spirit, and has committed himself to completing our transformation until Jesus returns for his children. We needn't be discouraged when we see clearly our own sin, our slow growth, or our clumsy faith. The Lord is the author of our faith. He is also the sustainer and finisher of our faith. He does not press pause on our sanctification because we've been lazy or bad, too angry or apathetic. He does not roll his eyes in disgust when we pass another day without reading the Bible. He draws us to himself, using whatever means necessary. He sees us, knows us, and loves us, moving us closer to perfect union with him and remaking us in his image.

Philippians 1:7–11. Paul continued his declaration of affection for these saints. They had supported him whether he was doing active ministry or suffering in prison because of it. The support these brothers and sisters sent was not contingent on some perception of "success," on the number of conversions or new small groups. Rather, they were committed to Paul and to the spread of the gospel because the Spirit lived in them.

As the church continued to pray for Paul, he continued to pray for them. Specifically, he prayed that their love would grow in certain qualities. We learn from this passage that Christian love is not rash, careless, or automatic. It discerns and tests, evaluates and thinks. Paul was asking that these believers would grow in their ability to assess what was needed for life in Christ.

Remember that the Philippian church was struggling in particular with unity. Surely Paul's specific prayer was targeting their disunity, one of Satan's favorite playgrounds in the church. Paul wanted these saints to have a love that was informed, smart, vigilant, and discerning. In Galatians 5:6 Paul wrote, "For in Christ Jesus neither circumcision nor uncircumcision counts for anything, but only faith working through love." It's as if he was directing these believers in how to love one another by saying, "Hey guys, you know that thing you keep arguing about and then talking about each other because of it, saying how wrong she was when she said x, y, or z? Winning the argument doesn't even matter. It doesn't even count. You know what does? Faith expressing itself through love for each other. I'm praying that your love grows in such a way that you figure out what counts."

Verses 10 and 11 show us that the goal of the love Paul wanted for these people was purity and blamelessness on the day when Christ returned. Paul wanted these believers to stand firmly in their faith, not to be blown around by useless arguments or heated, emotional discussions that didn't matter.

Paul loved the Philippian church deeply. He reminded them of who they were and told them of his consistent prayers for them, honoring them as partners in the gospel. He encouraged them with the knowledge that Christ would finish what he had begun in them, the work of the Spirit he had seen with his own eyes when he was among them. He poured out his affection for them and prayed for their maturity and wisdom. All of this he did with joy, even though he was in prison for believing what these brothers and sisters also believed. Surely the joy of the gospel is not bound by comfort. If the Spirit could awaken this kind of encouragement in Paul while he was awaiting trial and possible torture or death, the Spirit can work hope and energy into our hearts no matter our circumstance. Come, Holy Spirit, and let us know the joy of being in Christ.

Reflection Questions

4. Paul prayed with joy for the Philippians while he was imprisoned. How is this possible? What limits you personally from experiencing joy?

5. Verse 6 says God has started and will complete a good work in you. Where have you seen him in the process of completing a good work in you? How does that promise help you hope when you are struggling?

6. Part of Paul's prayer in verse 9 was for the church to have knowledge (facts, information, skills) and discernment (ability to perceive or judge well) in large amounts. What are you currently longing for knowledge and discernment about?

7. Paul's prayer was preparing the Philippians for the "day of Jesus Christ." How do you think a prayer like this adjusted the focus in this church?

8. Is there a current topic or area you are struggling to find unity about in your current church? In what ways has this passage reoriented your heart on this?

Focus verse

And I am sure of this, that he who began a good work in you will bring it to completion at the day of Jesus Christ.

Philippians 1:6

Reflections, curiosities, frustrations:

Study 2

Christ Is Proclaimed

Read Philippians 1:12–18

Observation Questions

1. What had been made known to the imperial guard?

2. What had Paul's imprisonment done for some brothers?

3. What are the two ways people were preaching Christ?

Interpretation

Philippians 1:12–14. The church at Philippi would have been praying regularly for their friend and mentor Paul. Letters and news about his progress could have only been delivered personally, by one of their own people. The Philippians finally received word that rather than growing the church and discipling people as they'd hoped, Paul had been captured and put into prison. What heartbreaking news! So much prayer, money, and hope for new believers and new churches had been expended. Out of their love for Jesus and their love for Paul, the Philippians gathered more money and sent one of their own members, Epaphroditus, to comfort Paul. They probably expected him to be discouraged—stuck in jail, in need of food and clothing, his mission on pause.

But the Paul Epaphroditus found was not discouraged; he was energized. The word translated "really" in verse 12 is a colloquial term that could also be translated "rather."[1] That is, *rather* than being a failed mission, what had happened to Paul served to advance the gospel. God was using Paul's stay in prison for the good of the kingdom. The Philippians learned that it was not that God was not answering their prayers. Instead, he was answering them in a way they had not and could not have anticipated. Is this not the way God works in our own lives at times? We pray for healing, and instead he grows us in endurance. We make plans to serve in a certain way or place, and he moves our hands to another. God will accomplish his mission. And he will do so using us. But we must never forget that he is the one who orders our steps and grows the seeds of the kingdom that we clumsily plant.

The Roman guard was probably not the target audience Paul was expecting. But they were the group of people God had chosen for Paul and his message. The guards, who were probably from the same group of the military whose job it was to protect the emperor and his family, all knew Paul was there because of Jesus. They probably worked in four-hour shifts, meaning at least twelve men were a regular captive audience of Paul. But there were probably others as well. As David Garland explains, "those with legal expertise who were working on the case or the Jewish lobby who brought the charges against Paul" would also have come into contact with Paul.[2]

Here was a group of influential people who had the ear of the emperor rubbing shoulders with Paul. Those in the church at Rome saw that God had dropped the master evangelist into the heart of the city. This strengthened the faith of the other Christians in Rome, giving them courage in the Lord to speak about him despite the danger. Nero was becoming more dangerous and more likely to punish anyone who wouldn't worship him, but God used Paul's prison term to embolden the believers in Rome. This is our God—unpredictable, unfettered, free. He is not bound by our plans or expectations or fears. He is not limited by the confines of our imagination.

Philippians 1:15–18. Paul was probably in prison either because Christianity was not an approved religion in Rome as Judaism had been or because officials were unsure as to whether followers of this religion could call Christ "Lord" in a place where they were politically required to call Caesar "Lord." You would think all Christians would come to comfort and encourage this man who was preaching Christ in such a hard place. But, no. Human hearts are capable of much evil. There were other believers in the city who were actually working against Paul, trying to make his stay in prison even more uncomfortable. Why would they do such a thing to this man some of them may have known personally?

It's possible that some believers were embarrassed by Paul's chains. Being imprisoned in the honor–shame culture of first-century Rome would have been a disgraceful thing. Others may have been envious of Paul's large influence in the Christian world. Whatever the reason, these men were out to hurt Paul. We would expect him to feel betrayed, angry, and bitter. And he probably was hurt; Paul was human after all.

Instead, we find Paul celebrating the fact that Christ was being preached, that the message was true, even if the motives of some preachers weren't pure or honorable. Paul's act of rejoicing in the midst of his difficult circumstances was not some autopilot reaction, no matter what he encountered. Rather, Paul was making a choice, born from years of suffering, made possible by kingdom priorities. Paul's greatest aim was the spread of the gospel; everything else was secondary.

And he was not necessarily married to his own plans for the way this work would get done. Of course he made plans, was strategic about his work in the church, and thought through his pastoral relationships. But Paul knew he was not ultimately in charge. Remember that Paul had called himself a "slave" of Jesus. This meant he would submit to his Lord even when nothing went the way he expected. Paul knew God could and would make disciples and build his kingdom through his people in the darkest of places and the strangest of circumstances.

This type of submission and trust flies in the face of our twenty-first-century individualistic program of happiness. It is offensive and foolish, in the eyes of most people, to endure harm or pain for the greater good. But Paul had been in Christ's school of suffering for years. He had learned to choose the kingdom and its joy instead of reacting to the roller coaster of circumstances. In fact, as we will see, Paul trusted that even his suffering would in the end be used for his good.

Reflection Questions

4. The Lord used Paul's imprisonment, a very difficult situation, to spread the gospel throughout the imperial guard, a wonderful result. When has God used a difficult situation in your life for a surprisingly good result? What currently is hard in your life that you can pray he will use in an impactful way like this?

5. "This is our God—unpredictable, unfettered, free. He is not bound by our plans or expectations or fears. He is not limited by the confines of our imagination." How have you found this to be true in your life?

6. In verses 15–18, we learn Paul was getting opposition, for unknown reasons, from his own brothers and sisters in Christ. Describe when you have felt such opposition with fellow believers and how that situation felt to you.

7. In verse 18, Paul ultimately celebrated Christ being proclaimed, no matter the motive. Is this surprising to you? Why or why not?

8. Even though God may not have grown the church in the ways Paul expected, Paul still trusted and submitted to God's plan as the best plan. When have you felt your plan is better than God's, making it hard to get on board with God's plan? What did you learn from that?

Focus verse

What then? Only that in every way, whether in pretense or in truth, Christ is proclaimed, and in that I rejoice.

Philippians 1:18

Reflections, curiosities, frustrations:

Study 3

Sharing in Christ's Suffering

Read Philippians 1:19–30

Observation Questions

1. What was Paul hoping for in verse 20?

2. What are the two things Paul is wrestling between in verses 21–26?

3. According to verses 27 and 28, what did Paul want to be true of the Philippians?

Interpretation

Philippians 1:19–20. Here Paul tells us the secret behind his joy and confident hope of deliverance. It's not that he was working harder, had the right connections, was carefully planning, or was making sure he kept everyone around him happy. None of those things were reliable predictors of a good future. None of those guaranteed his deliverance, either from the jail he was currently in or from death itself, which was not out of the question if his trial went badly. Paul was relying on two things for a hopeful future: the prayers of the church and the Holy Spirit. These things made up his strategy.

Execution was a real possibility for Paul, though he was not necessarily expecting that as the outcome of his trial. Even in this context, Paul had the audacity to expect that, whether he lived or died, he would be able to honor Christ, to magnify him publicly. Where can we find the confidence of Paul? How can we know that no matter our circumstances, we will boldly glorify Jesus as we grow in our faith? This is only possible for us in the same way it was possible for Paul—through the prayers of our brothers and sisters and the work of the Holy

Spirit. Contrary to what we hear every day in our culture, we were not made to live independent lives, cutting our paths apart from everyone else, islands of strength as we make our own way in the world. We were actually created to be dependent both on God and on others. We were crafted in such a way that we cannot live wholeheartedly without needing God and needing people around us. This was not a mistake by our Creator but a purposeful weaving and integration of community. Therefore, all of life, and especially our spiritual life, is to be lived dependently. Our sanctification is not to be "just me and Jesus" but "me within the church of Jesus" as a path to growth and change.

Philippians 1:21–26. Here again we see Paul putting aside his own preferences for those of the kingdom. Remember that he was writing to a divided church. He used his own hypothetical choice (though he didn't really have a choice) of life or death. Clearly, death was his preference. The place where souls rest until Jesus comes to judge all and end the world as we know it is often referred to as the "intermediate state." Paul knew he would see Jesus face to face and be free of all of the fetters of sin and pain if he went there. But Paul gave these divided, probably frustrated men and women an example to follow. In this hypothetical choice, he willingly put aside his own desire and chose to "remain in the flesh" for the sake of the Philippians and their faith and growth. He knew he could serve, love, and teach them while on earth, doing fruitful ministry among them and others. He put their good above his own.

 Verse 21 is a litmus test for our hearts. Is life for us a matter of honoring Jesus (verse 20)—literally, "enlarging" or "magnifying" him? Or is he a comfortable add-on or useful app we turn to when needed? If he were to end our lives today and call us to full and immediate communion with him, would we consider that progress or a benefit for us, better than our lives now? Idolatry steals away the freedom of joyfully answering yes to these questions.

Philippians 1:27–30. In verse 27, the word that is translated as "let your manner be," literally means "live as citizens." But here Paul added the word "worthy."[1] We could read this verse like this: "Only live as worthy citizens of the gospel of Christ." Citizenship in Philippi was a big deal in Paul's day. In fact, a Philippian citizen enjoyed all the rights and privileges of a Roman citizen, a coveted position in the ancient world. These rights would have included voting, standing for public office, and immunity from some taxes. Paul was reminding these believers that just as they were citizens of Rome with its responsibilities and privileges, so too they were citizens of heaven. Their lives needed to reflect this.

Paul intended to send the letter ahead to Philippi and then come himself. But before he arrived, he wanted to hear that the Philippians were contending together, working as one body. Their unity and refusal to shrink back from their enemies and opposition would be proof, said Paul, of their enemies' ultimate judgment by Christ and the church's ultimate salvation. Apparently, the Christians were being punished for their allegiance to the Lord Jesus instead of the lord emperor. Paul was probably in prison for the same reason. Roman citizens would have somehow honored the current emperor at public events. It's possible that the Christians' refusal to show reverence in the prescribed way was causing them serious trouble.

Paul did not tell these brothers and sisters to hope the struggle would go away or to pray that God would keep them from any more hardship. Paul told them that living as people who would name only Jesus as their Lord in a time and place where their culture was punishing them for doing so was a special privilege, a gift from God. How? we might ask. For the Christian, the path to splendor must first always go through struggle. Death must always come before life. This is the consistent rhythm of the life of a disciple: death, then life. As Moisés Silva writes, "Suffering is the way to glory, God's gift of salvation for his children."[2]

Paul was speaking specifically here of suffering for Christ and claiming allegiance to him as Lord. For the Philippians and for us, suffering is not a sign of punishment or that God has turned away. Rather, it is a special gift for us to be able to share in the fellowship of suffering with Christ. We in the western church do not presently experience the suffering that our brothers and sisters do in some parts of the world. But the little that we may suffer here and there because of our allegiance to Christ must be counted as a benefit, not a loss. If you ever doubt this, consider some of the "rock stars" of the faith, if you will. Peter was crucified upside down. Paul was beaten, imprisoned, poor, and misunderstood. Stephen was stoned to death. These are the privileged, the exceptional, the honored. What does this tell you about the life to which Jesus is calling you? It is a life of sacrifice, a call to come and die.

Reflection Questions

4. Paul was dependent on the prayers of other believers and the Holy Spirit to give him joy and sustain him through all circumstances. Do you recognize your dependence on these things? Why or why not?

5. Paul was putting aside his preference of dying and being with Christ in order to remain on earth to be helpful to the church. Where are you currently putting aside your preferences or desires in order to do something greater that the Lord has called you to?

6. When have you ever suffered for the sake of Christ? Did you consider it a gift or a burden?

7. What about the concept of suffering for Christ feels intimidating or over-whelming to you? Why?

8. When you are suffering do you tend to pray it will go away? How has Paul's perspective in this passage shifted how you want to approach suffering?

Focus verse

For it has been granted to you that for the sake of Christ you should not only believe in him but also suffer for his sake.

Philippians 1:29

Reflections, curiosities, frustrations:

Study 4

The Name Above Every Name

Read Philippians 2:1–11

Observation Questions

1. What are the things Paul listed in verse 1 that should have motivated the church in Philippi?

2. In verses 2–5 what was Paul calling the Philippians to?

3. In verses 6–8 how did Paul describe the actions of Jesus?

Interpretation

As we begin reading a new chapter, it's important to remember that this is a letter, meant to be read all at once in one sitting. Therefore, we must begin reading chapter 2 with the context of chapter 1 squarely in our minds. Though much of these first four verses could be applied to our lives as Christians in general, Paul wrote these instructions and commands to a divided church as an antidote to the fighting going on there.

Philippians 2:1. It is easy to read the "you" in this verse as a second-person singular pronoun, leading to a me-and-Jesus, individualized perspective. But Paul intended for the entire sentence to speak to the church as a whole; he was addressing the Philippian church as a body—second-person plural, "you all." When he wrote of encouragement, comfort, fellowship, and tenderness, he meant that which they had received from God through one another. Sanctification (growing in Christ) and glorification (final, total unity with Christ) are corporate endeavors. We are saved into the body, we grow as the body, and we will one day gather around the throne of Jesus to worship as a body.

Philippians 2:2. Paul's "if" in verse 1 is better translated "since." *Since* you've experienced all these things within the church, you must do what I'm asking. And what was he asking? That they be unified in all things. The word translated "complete" is used in Romans and in 2 Timothy to mean "to fill someone up with something." Paul told the church to fill him up with joy by being unified in every way. He called them, in this place of division, to have one mind and one purpose, to move as a unit. What do these words look like lived out, with skin on? The next fifteen verses describe exactly that.

Philippians 2:3. Paul put together two words to construct what we read in English as "vain conceit": *kenos* (empty) + *doxa* (glory) = empty glory. This is the craving of reputation and greatness that surrounded these saints in Roman culture. Status was a big deal and included everything from family origin to wealth, intelligence, and speaking ability. This hunger for prestige and position had crept into the church at Philippi and was destroying the unity of the body. Most of us, unfortunately, could describe our own experiences of this in the church, whether brought about by our own vanity and selfishness or by that of another.

Here Paul was calling the believers, and subsequently us, to be fundamentally different from the surrounding culture. Instead of valuing their own status or reputation, these men and women needed to pursue humility. In their culture, humility was something reserved for slaves, outcasts, and people with no reputation at all. But the character of the kingdom of God is not the same as that of first-century Rome or Philippi or of the United States in the twenty-first century. In the kingdom, we put others first. We consider others better, not in our assessment of them, but in our consideration of their needs and rights.

Philippians 2:4. We should attempt to care for all of the interests of brothers and sisters. Yes, Jesus told us, you are your brother's keeper. Paul was not commanding these people to be doormats or to neglect self-care. He was warning against self-centeredness. The church at Philippi was a product, at least partially, of its culture, where phrases like "look after your own things" and "do good to yourself" were everywhere.[1] Our culture is not so different. "Treat yourself" and "you deserve it" are mantras of the current western world. We, as daughters and sons of the King, are called to embody a different ethic.

Philippians 2:5–8. Though scholars still debate whether these verses were a hymn that already existed in the early church, Paul made his theology clear here. Jesus, our elder brother, is a self-sacrificing lover of people who willingly put privilege aside to liberate those he loved.

But first, where did Jesus begin? As the sovereign, the ruler God himself. He had every advantage in existence. He gave orders to the morning, showed the dawn its place, and said to the sea, "Thus far you shall come, and no farther" (Job 38:11). There is no power or authority available that he did not already possess. Therefore, no one could ever coerce him into giving anything away. Whatever he did, he did willingly, as the one who rules. Instead of protecting his privileges, he chose to lay them down, setting them aside. He stepped down, condescended, relinquished his power.

He made himself nothing. Literally, he emptied himself. This was not a change in his essential nature. His "God-ness" did not and could not be changed. Rather, this was a change in his role, a voluntary shift in his status. Notice the pattern:

down, down, down. Down from the ultimate status of almighty to that of a man. Down from omnipotence and blinding glory to the limitations of a human body—hunger, fatigue, disease. He was born in the likeness of men, fully human but without sin. And his condescension didn't stop at the incarnation. As a human, he chose the place of a servant. Jesus submitted himself to a mother's authority, to Roman laws, to temple rules. He became obedient, voluntarily limiting the exercise of his rightful authority, to the point of being forsaken, killed. Lower, lower, lower.

Jesus did not die in an honorable way like a brave soldier or a good citizen dying for his cause. There was neither dignity in his death nor celebration of his life. Crucifixion was reserved for slaves and thieves. Even in his death he took the lowest place. His death was the opposite of what the Romans would have counted as noble, the opposite of the vain glory against which Paul warned these believers. This is the ethic of the kingdom—enduring shame and weakness; dependence, humility, and yielding. This is the pattern of the Christian life, and it is what Jesus calls us to. First we must realize what privileges we've been given in this world. In what arenas do we have pull or advantage? Where does our privilege protect us, our status save us? Paul commanded the Philippians to put all advantage aside for the sake of their brothers and sisters, especially during conflict. This is God's call to us in the midst of disagreement in the church. Christ the King who condescended for our good asks us to do the same for others.

Philippians 2:9–11. But stopping there is like closing the book after the crucifixion. It's not over! The rhythm of the believing life is always death then life, burial then resurrection, a kernel of wheat falling to the ground and dying to produce many seeds. Jesus's absolute humiliation was followed by supreme exaltation. There is not a more prestigious name than his—and a name in Semitic culture meant more than just what you called someone. It was your capacity, your job, your basis for existence. Jesus alone now holds this place and name. God put him there in response to his self-sacrifice.

Paul makes clear reference in verse 10 to Isaiah 45:22–23, where we read, "Turn to me and be saved, all the ends of the earth! For I am God, and there is no other. By myself I have sworn; from my mouth has gone out in righteousness a word that shall not return: 'To me every knee shall bow, every tongue shall swear allegiance.'" Jesus was being named as the Lord and God, the only God. If they had not yet understood Jesus's equality with the God of the Old Testament Israel up to this point, they couldn't miss it here. Paul explained that all those now living and those dead, all angels and all demons will one day bow. He was not predicting mass conversion, confession that leads to repentance. Rather, he explained, all will finally admit Jesus's true identity and authority. Some will do so with joy; others will surely do so on their way to agony. Even those who were opposing these brothers and sisters in Philippi will bow in deferential respect before the Lord.

Remember again the context—division, persecution, and suffering. This little church needed to hear that at the end of the day, when all of the battles were over and powers that seemed so unmovable on this earth were made to finally come face to face with the Lord, none would be left standing. All would bow to the true King. For us, the message is the same. All who work with us; all who work against us; every friend and enemy; teachers, mothers, pastors, friends, and children—all will take the posture of a servant and say the words with their lips that they have been made to say: "You are the Lord. There is no other."

Reflection Questions

4. What does unity in the church look like? What makes you resist unity with your brothers and sisters? What helps you lean into it?

5. What does it look like to live other-centered lives considering others' needs and rights? What is the hardest part of that for you?

6. Jesus was placed in human history with no power, a servant, someone who had to submit to authority in every area of his life, someone whose status followed a pattern of down, down, down. How does this affect your view of his sacrifice for us? Your view of humility?

7. Paul wanted the Philippians to let the mindset of Christ shape how they interacted with others in the church. What might you need to repent of currently in this area?

8. Paul described a day when every person and authority will submit to the name of Christ. What do you visualize when you think about this moment?

Focus verse

Therefore God has highly exalted him and bestowed on him the name that is above every name, so that at the name of Jesus every knee should bow, in heaven and on earth and under the earth.

Philippians 2:9–10

Reflections, curiosities, frustrations:

Study 5

God Works in You

Read Philippians 2:12–18

Observation Questions

1. According to verse 13, who is working in you and for what purpose?

2. Define the words "grumbling" and "disputing."

3. According to verses 15–16, what did Paul hope the Philippians would become?

Interpretation

Philippians 2:12–13. Before we start discussing this passage, let's make a helpful distinction between Paul's purpose in his letters to the Romans and to the Galatians and his point here. Romans 11:6 reads, "But if it is by grace, it is no longer on the basis of works; otherwise grace would no longer be grace." Galatians 2:16 says, "Yet we know that a person is not justified by works of the law but through faith in Jesus Christ, so we also have believed in Christ Jesus, in order to be justified by faith in Christ and not by works of the law, because by works of the law no one will be justified."

In Romans and Galatians, Paul was explaining how a person is saved—the means by which a person receives salvation. It is by grace through faith; it cannot be earned. Good works cannot buy salvation. But that's not the point Paul was making in Philippians 2. Here he was writing to believers who already understood grace through faith. The means of salvation was not the issue they were struggling with. Instead, Paul the pastor spoke directly to their need, exhorting them to follow the example of their master. He told them to practice humility as a prescription for the division happening in their church. He was showing them how to work out their salvation. These people had already been saved. Paul was telling them what to do with their salvation. As he wrote in Ephesians 2:10, "For we are his workmanship, created in Christ Jesus for good works, which God prepared beforehand, that we should walk in them." We are saved *for* good works, not *by* good works.

Paul knew his friends were suffering, so he encouraged them. The real power behind his encouragement came in verse 13, when he told them that they worked because God works. God was empowering them, energizing them, giving them the will to work. Because God works, they could work. And so Paul could freely say to them, "Work out your salvation. Walk it out. Be obedient." Notice that the attitude the Philippians were to have, and we are to have as we do this work, is one of fear and trembling, in awe of God and in submission to one another. Here again we see that the "your" in the phrase "work out your salvation" is plural.

Our salvation is not individual but corporate; we're saved into a body. We also work out our salvation together. So that girl who drives you crazy with all of her drama? How you respond to her is part of you working out your salvation. The lady who seems to always be telling you she's praying for you? Letting her do so, and telling her what you need prayer for, is part of working it out. The child that drives you to your knees over and over? Bringing your anxiety to the Lord is working it out. All of these things are part of walking out what God has already given to us, in all of our weakness and stumbling. We work because God works first.

Philippians 2:14–16. "You sound like the Israelites, grumbling in the wilderness," said Paul. "They were supposed to be a light to the nations; now you should be that light. All of your bickering is affecting your witness." The grumbling Paul described was that quiet, mouth-covered, head-turned grumbling at the back of the meeting. It was the muttering against leaders, the fighting and complaining.

These were not the bright and honorable actions of those who "shine as lights in the world." The way the Philippians treated one another mattered. Our behavior is noticed by our surrounding culture. Of course, there are always things to complain about in the church; it is full of broken people. Part of faithfulness looks like knowing when to hold our tongues.

Philippians 2:17–18. Levitical priests would have poured out a wine offering in the sanctuary, according to God's command (Numbers 28:7). Paul is comparing himself to this sacrifice as he suffered as a prisoner. But he was not depressed or hopeless; nor did he want his friends to be so. Instead, he told them to rejoice. But why? Isn't this the opposite of what we would expect Paul to do?

Remember how Paul started this letter. Because of his imprisonment, others were hearing the gospel and the Roman church had been emboldened. Because of these things, he rejoiced. The final result for Paul and his beloved Philippian church was already known—glory. He referred to the day of Christ in passing because it was already a guarantee. Their end would be never-ending joy. Because of this, he was free to rejoice in the midst of prison and uncertainty. As Gordon Fee writes, "Joy has nothing to do with circumstances, but everything to do with one's place in Christ."[1] Paul was showing his brothers and sisters, and therefore us, the path of joy in the midst of suffering. Our place in Christ is the only thing that can enable us to rejoice while we suffer in this world.

Reflection Questions

4. What is your reaction to this statement: "We are saved *for* good works, not *by* good works"?

5. How have you seen God use the community of Christians to work out his purposes in your life and in the lives of others?

6. Think about the idea that God is always working in you to accomplish his will and good pleasure for the body as a whole. How does this change your view of certain circumstances in your life right now?

7. Where are you currently having a hard time not grumbling or disputing with your fellow brother or sister in Christ? What are the possible implications of that for those around you inside and outside the church?

8. The call on Paul's life was so hard that he could not rely on circumstances as his main source of joy. Instead he drew joy from his place in Christ. What are some practical ways you can look past your life circumstances to draw from this steady, unshakable joy?

Focus verse

For it is God who works in you, both to will and work for his good pleasure.

Philippians 2:13

Reflections, curiosities, frustrations:

Study 6
Fellow Workers

Read Philippians 2:19–30

Observation Questions

1. How did Paul describe Timothy in verses 19–23?

2. How did Paul describe Epaphroditus in verses 25–30?

3, What appears to be Paul's hope in sending these two men to the Philippians?

Interpretation

Philippians 2:19–21. It may seem upon a first reading of this passage that we've gone from inspiring metaphors of holiness and sacrifice to mundane travel plans. But don't miss what Paul was doing here. In making plans to send Timothy and Epaphroditus, he was doing exactly what he required of the Philippians—putting others' needs above his own. This is what working out his salvation looked like for Paul. This is what it is to "look not only to your own interests but also to the interests of others." Paul was the one under house arrest, awaiting news of his own trial. Yet his intention was to send his two partners back to the Philippian church. Yes, sending Timothy was partially for Paul's encouragement, to eventually get a report about the church's growth and faithfulness. But these two men were living examples of the humility described in Philippians 2:5–11, and they would be helpful to the Philippian church in their struggle with disunity.

Paul described Timothy as being "like-souled."[1] He contrasted Timothy with those he mentioned in Philippians 1:17, the ones who were preaching Christ out of selfish ambition. They were the "all" he referred to here in verse 21. Of course, not every Christian in Rome was insincere. Paul was using hyperbole, a rhetorical tool, to call attention to Timothy as one to be emulated.

Philippians 2:22–24. Paul continued to lay out Timothy's credentials. In his day, telling a son that he seemed to care about the same things his dad cared about was a huge compliment. Timothy had devoted himself to caring about the things of God, thus proving himself to be a good pastor. Paul felt confident in his plan to send Timothy in his stead.

Philippians 2:25–28. But before Timothy, Paul would send this letter with Epaphroditus. Don't get lost in the logistics or names here, but follow Paul into these personal, tender moments in the life of the church. Epaphroditus's name was probably some form of the Greek goddess Aphrodite, goddess of love, beauty, pleasure, and procreation. He was probably a converted pagan who had grown to be a faithful and trusted brother in the church. He was sent by the church in Philippi to give Paul food, money, warm clothes, and encouragement. Remember that these were not the eight hundred– or even three hundred–member churches of today. This was 60 or 62 A.D. The church worldwide was not yet thirty years old. The church in Philippi was probably only about fifteen to twenty years old, and not very large.

Everyone would have at least known Paul's name, and all would have known Epaphroditus personally. They would have pooled together what they could and sent him out, after much prayer and probably tears, onto a dangerous journey to try to encourage, feed, and clothe their father in the faith. But on the way, Epaphroditus contracted some sort of life-threatening illness, and there would have been no quick antibiotic at the local urgent care clinic for it. Their beloved brother almost died. In the Greek he was literally "next door neighbor" to death.[2]

Imagine Paul caring for Epaphroditus on his deathbed, dreading the loss of a trusted friend and co-worker as he awaited what could have been his own death sentence. Think of those in Philippi who had heard rumors of Epaphroditus's illness worrying and praying for him. There was no text, email, or phone that could reassure them of his eventual recovery. Letters were delivered by hand and took weeks to arrive. No wonder Paul wanted to send Epaphroditus himself with the letter, commending him as a fellow soldier in the spiritual war of the gospel. Paul knew the church was worried, and he wanted them to welcome Epaphroditus as they should, a fellow slave who was willing to die for the sake of others.

Philippians 2:29–30. Notice the appearance of the word "joy" again. Paul was reframing this brother's homecoming for the church. It could have easily felt like what had happened was a failure—a shortened visit fraught with deathbed sorrow. But Paul directed them again toward joy, because Epaphroditus did for him what the Philippians couldn't do because of their geographical distance.

It is easy to read these words from a cold, distant perspective, like a history textbook, full of long-dead, foreign people. But these were real people with friendships, family, habits, favorite foods, sleep problems, bad knees, and close confidants. They missed each other, prayed for each other, and relied on each other. Paul knew what was true and is still true today; we need examples to follow, people to imitate. We need to see what it looks like to walk out and work out our salvation. We need flesh and blood examples that look like our ultimate example, who in the most perfect way looked not only to his own interests but also to the interests of others.

Reflection Questions

4. Paul was in his own state of need and suffering but decided to serve the church in Philippi by sending these two partners of his to care for them. When have you had someone sacrifice for you even during a difficult time in their own life?

5. Paul had a deep bond with Timothy and described him as being "like-souled." Where in the church have you experienced a similar level of friendship and like-mindedness? What effect has it had on you and those around you?

6. Paul talked about God's mercy in sparing Epaphroditus's life and how that spared Paul from "sorrow upon sorrow." Can you relate to Paul with an experience of God sparing a friend of yours from death that was a mercy to you? Describe that situation.

7. Again Paul called the Philippians to joy despite their less than ideal circumstances. What attitude instead of joy would your heart be tempted to have if you were in a similar situation? Why?

8. What is your reaction to hearing about these men and their very real and deep relationship with each other? What does it make you want to hope and pray for in your own life?

Focus verse

I am the more eager to send him, therefore, that you may rejoice at seeing him again, and that I may be less anxious.

Philippians 2:28

Reflections, curiosities, frustrations:

Study 7

The Surpassing Worth of Knowing Christ

Read Philippians 3:1–11

Observation Questions

1. In verses 2–3, whom did Paul tell the Philippians to look out for? Why?

2. According to verses 4–6, what things could Paul have confidence in?

3. What did Paul say in verses 7–11 was worth more than his accomplishments? What did he say he gained from knowing Christ?

Interpretation

Philippians 3:1–3. Paul didn't use "finally" to mean he was approaching the end of his letter. It's more like, "as for the other matters we need to talk about…" This word is a transition from one topic to another. But before he launched into a warning, he reminded the Philippians of the way to walk through their suffering: by rejoicing. This wasn't Paul flippantly telling these friends to put a positive spin on a negative emotion. In fact, it was not passive at all. This is an imperative, a command. It's something he wanted them to do in the midst of their trials. To rejoice means to praise, to sing, to name the good things about God. It's the drum Paul kept beating because he knew it was what these Christian believers needed to help them persevere—to remind themselves of who God was and whose they were. As David Chapman writes, "Joy is a choice. It is a commitment to rejoice in our relationship to Christ and our identity in him."[1]

Next, a warning. Paul warned these dear brothers and sisters about the Judaizers. These Jews who had been converted to Christianity believed Gentile converts had to obey the Torah (Old Testament law) and be circumcised, effectively becoming Jews culturally before they could be real Christians. Paul used strong language to warn the Philippians about these people, saying: "Watch out! These people want you to believe you must add something to Christ's righteousness. They're dangerous." Though they had not necessarily gained influence in Philippi, Paul had encountered Judaizers before in various cities, and he anticipated them trying to convince the Gentiles in the church there to be circumcised.

What was so dangerous? Would it have really been so bad to circumcise the Gentile believers? It certainly would have made the Jewish Christians more comfortable. It may have even spared some in the church persecution since Jews were more accepted than Christians in the culture. The problem was these Christians were telling Gentiles they had to do something outwardly to qualify for grace. They had to take one more step to right themselves before the righteousness of Christ could be enough. This is not the gospel at all.

And so Paul called them dogs, which is what Jews normally called Gentiles. He called them evildoers because instead of teaching others to rest in the righteousness of Jesus, they pushed Gentiles to add some external act to their faith. He called them mutilators—literally, "those who cut to pieces," a play on the idea of circumcision—because they had become no better than those who cut on flesh as in a pagan ritual. They had it all upside down, he told the Philippians. Circumcision pointed to something else, and that something was circumcision of the heart. Both the former Jews and the Gentiles who worshipped by the Spirit gave glory to Jesus. We are the true circumcision. We put our confidence not in a physical act, but in Christ.

Philippians 3:4–6. Paul knew his resume meant nothing for the kingdom. So in a moment of sarcasm, it is as if he was saying, "Oh, you wanna play that game? You wanna play the 'who has more reasons to be confident in what they've done externally' game? Let me give you my list. I was circumcised before those people even knew who Jesus was. I'm from the holiest tribe, raised by two Hebrew-speaking Jews, a member of the most rigorous sect who actually call themselves 'the separated ones,' trained in both the written and oral law by the best of the best. I was ahead of everyone my age in terms of punishing those who didn't keep the Jewish law, including having Christians killed. And I kept that law to a T, down to the last detail. When it comes to the type of righteousness the Judaizers can offer you, I can play this game better than anyone else can. Bring it."

Philippians 3:7–8. Although Paul knew he could play the comparison game in Jewish outward righteousness and win, he also knew the game was meaningless. When he encountered Christ on the road to Damascus, he saw clearly that all of his credentials and zeal to work for God's acceptance were not actually advantages. Instead of points that helped gain God's affection, they were losses. Everything he thought was moving him into a better status with God was actually working against him. Why? Because these things "had in reality been working to destroy him because they were blinding him to his need for the real righteousness which God required."[2] Only by renouncing the things we think earn us God's favor can we begin to find righteousness in Christ. The things Paul counted as gain were not bad in and of themselves, but using them as the grounds for his status before God was useless. Paul really did suffer loss. He had an amazing reputation and a bright future being honored in the Jewish community. He was an up-and-coming young Pharisee. But compared to knowing Jesus, all his former advantages he called rubbish—literally, "human feces." A new perspective came into place for Paul when he met Christ. Knowing Jesus, for Paul, was not an intellectual exercise or mental assent. This knowing was the knowing between a husband and wife; it was intimate and personal. It had a history. And its glory far surpassed anything he had ever known.

Philippians 3:9–11. Paul recognized that his righteousness came only from being in Christ, in union with him, which happens through faith. This rightness, this right standing with God, was given to him, to the Philippians, and therefore to us, by God. As Gordon Fee explains, "Grace plus anything cancels out grace."[3] This is something that God grants, that God does. We cannot reverse it, add to it, or diminish it any more than we can undo Christ's resurrection. This means that when we've ignored God, ignored his Word, spoken harshly to our children, been cruel to our husbands, or sinned in various other ways, God's opinion of us does not change. It also means we cannot make him love or accept us any more than he already does by giving more money, holding our tongue, teaching Sunday school, or reading our Bibles. If our standing depends on Jesus's record, which is finished, then God's opinion of us is fixed, reliable, unchanged.

Paul knew Christ. But he wanted more. He knew that as God used him in kingdom work and made him more like Jesus, he used suffering to do so. Jesus's resurrection came only after his suffering on the cross. His followers should expect the same patterns. Knowing Jesus intimately means knowing his experience of sacrifice and death to self. Paul longed for even deeper intimacy with Christ, which only comes through life with the same pattern—rejoicing in our relationship to Christ in the midst of our suffering.

Reflection Questions

4. In verse 1, Paul didn't merely suggest but commanded his readers to rejoice, or to praise, to sing, to name the good things about God. Have you ever tried to do this when you felt no joy? What resulted?

5. Paul was strongly warning the church that believers who suggested something needs to be added to Christ's righteousness were dangerous. How has this been dangerous in your own life?

6. Paul had quite a religious "resume" in which he could rest. What's on your Christian resume? How could you, like Paul, shift your thinking on this?

7. "Grace plus anything cancels out grace." What is your "plus anything"?

8. Our standing with God is secure, stable, and unshakably based on Jesus's behavior and obedience in our place. What is the impact of this truth on your relationship with God?

Focus verse

Indeed, I count everything as loss because of the surpassing worth of knowing Christ Jesus my Lord. For his sake I have suffered the loss of all things and count them as rubbish, in order that I may gain Christ.

Philippians 3:8

Reflections, curiosities, frustrations:

Study 8

We Await a Savior

Read Philippians 3:12–21

Observation Questions

1. Did Paul consider himself already perfect?

2. What way of thinking did Paul live by according to verses 13–15?

3. In verses 18–19, how did Paul describe those who were "enemies of the cross of Christ"?

Interpretation

Philippians 3:12–13. What is the "this" to which Paul referred in verse 12? All of the things he just mentioned in verses 10–11: knowing Christ and the power of his resurrection, sharing in his sufferings, becoming like him in his death. Paul was talking about the already–not yet of this world. The kingdom of God is already in place, but it has not yet come in its fullness, as it will when he returns. Therefore, Christ's work in Paul had not yet reached its completion, when he will be perfect, not in the moral sense, but in the sense of being fully mature. Paul was still a sinner, still struggling with obedience. But as he struggled, he pushed forward in his walk, forcing himself to keep going. Like a runner nearing the finish line of the race, he strained himself, leaning toward the last step.

Philippians 3:14–15. The image of a race continues. Picture a starting line full of runners. A gun is fired, and in a flurry of breath and movement, they leap off the line, find their pace, and set their eyes on the finish line. Those who finish well receive their prize. In our race, the gun that signals the start is the call of God to salvation. The call Paul spoke of here is not to a particular vocation or particular action. It is the summons of Jesus to his children to come to him, to abide in him, to be his. And what is the prize at the end of this race? There are many, including a resurrected body, eternal life, and rewards. But the most precious prize is perfect, unimpeded fellowship with Jesus. All of the wondering about whether he hears, whether he sees, will be over. All of the longing to see him, touch him, really know him and be known fully, will end. All of the struggle to obey, to be like him, to be undistracted by the things of this world, will be finished. We will be with him fully, permanently.

Philippians 3:16–19. Paul was absolutely sure of this model, this pattern, this way of life for the believer. He had confidence that those who belonged to God would eventually see life in the same way. For now, he urged them, and us, to live up to—literally, "get in line with" or "be guided by"—what we have already attained. And what is that? We have attained the righteousness of Christ, which, as David Garland writes, "excludes all boasting, vanity, and haughtiness toward others."[1]

We should follow the example of Paul in his dependence on Jesus. And not just the example of Paul but also of Timothy and Epaphroditus, who were well known to the Philippians. And not just of them but of mature Christians all around us. There is a recognizable path, a template of the cruciform life, that is, a pattern of life shaped by the cross. And there are people around us, as there were for Paul, who walk this path. We are to identify them and imitate them, because in them, as Sinclair Ferguson writes, "the pattern of Christ's own life is reproduced."[2]

What about those who claim to be Christians but don't live out this pattern? Paul spoke heavy words about these people, calling them enemies of the cross. They lived no differently than pagans, claiming the name of Jesus but refusing to live like their master. Instead of being ruled by Christ and his kingdom as their priority, they were ruled by the "stomach" or "flesh." They lived self-centered lives, always looking for comfort and pleasure.

Philippians 3:20–21. Some of the brothers and sisters in Philippi were actually Roman citizens, having all the rights and privileges of a person living in Rome.

They understood themselves to be an outpost of another kingdom, with their true citizenship in another place. This is exactly what Paul pointed to as he said that in the same way, their true citizenship was not on this earth but in another place. Their genuine home, their legitimate allegiance, their proper resting place was heaven. No wonder they felt and we feel so out of place here sometimes! Deep in our souls we know this is not the way things are supposed to be. We long for things to be made right, to be fully satisfied and completely content. This isn't just a spiritual longing but also a physical one. And Jesus will transform our "lowly body" to be like his. This is not a statement about flesh being bad and spirit good. Rather, Paul was saying our current bodies would die because of the effects of sin, but we will follow our elder brother and be given a new, resurrected body, free of pain, disease, and death. How? By the same power that was given to Jesus by the Father. Jesus is the prize at the end of this race, and he is worth the running.

Reflection Questions

4. Is it comforting to think about Paul still struggling with sin and not having reached perfection in this life? Why or why not?

5. "All of the wondering about whether he hears, whether he sees will be over. All of the longing to see him, touch him, really know him and be known fully will end. All of the struggle to obey, to be like him, to be undistracted by the things of this world will be finished." Which part of this picture of heaven are you most excited for?

6. Who are the mature Christians currently in your life? What have you learned by watching them?

7. In verse 19, Paul gave this description of those claiming to be Christians but aren't: "Their end is destruction, their god is their belly, and they glory in their shame, with minds set on earthly things." What are some concrete examples of what this looks like?

8. Like the Philippians, we are dual citizens of this world and the kingdom of God. Where in your life do you feel this tension most?

Focus verse

But our citizenship is in heaven, and from it we await a Savior, the Lord Jesus Christ, who will transform our lowly body to be like his glorious body, by the power that enables him even to subject all things to himself.

Philippians 3:20–21

Reflections, curiosities, frustrations:

Study 9

Rejoice in the Lord Always

Read Philippians 4:1–9

Observation Questions

1. What did Paul ask of Euodia and Syntyche?

2. What did Paul ask the Philippians to do instead of being anxious?

3. What are the eight things Paul asked the Philippians to think about in verse 8?

Interpretation

Philippians 4:1–3. Paul's affection for his spiritual children could not be contained. Their maturity was his reward. He bridged his previous teaching to his next bold words with this display of tenderness. And then came the moment of truth, the words for which some commentators think this entire letter was preparing. Paul publicly called out two prominent women of the church, begging them to agree. He used the same word he used in Philippians 2:2, urging them to be "of the same mind." These two women's serious disagreement could possibly have been the beginning and core of the church's disunity. Paul didn't mince words. He spent three chapters explaining the way of self-sacrifice to prepare them to hear him beg for their reconciliation.

Euodia (meaning "success") and Syntyche (meaning "lucky") had pagan names and were probably early Gentile converts. These were not outside, fringey troublemakers. They were pillars of the church, fellow workers with Paul. They were respected, believing women who had a disagreement. They probably fought about some practical outworking of their shared faith. But their clash grew, people took sides, and bitterness and resentment spread. The repercussions of their conflict were large and dangerous. Paul did not shame or dismiss these women. Nor did he discuss particulars. He asked the church to help them, dignifying them with descriptors along the way. Love doesn't skirt around uncomfortable situations; nor does it blow them out of proportion. It tenderly entreats the body to help. Why? Because, as Sinclair Ferguson writes, "Paul makes clear that division between two individuals in a Christian fellowship can never remain a private matter between them. It inevitably affects others."[1]

Philippians 4:4–6. As he had before, Paul commanded the Philippians to rejoice. Paul was not asking these saints to drum up an emotion. Christian rejoicing is something we must practice, like gratitude. It is an attitude, a posture, a point of view. To rejoice in the Lord means that despite what we see around us, we can choose to let what God says be the most influential truth in our lives. Paul was, in effect, telling these believers to meditate on what God has said. The Lord will return, he reminded them. And how foolish would they feel if they were found arguing about trivial practicalities when he did? Paul knew those in Philippi lived under the daily stress of persecution and fear, so he spoke directly to that fear, telling them to replace their anxiety with thankful prayer. Instead of letting their anxiety distract them or pull them apart, they were to name all of their needs to God and wait in dependence on him to provide.

Philippians 4:7–9. Easier said than done, right? It's true that committing our needs to prayer instead of mulling them over in our anxiety is difficult to do consistently. But Paul gave us three encouraging words about this anxiety we all fight. First, he promised God's peace, explaining its presence like a fortress where one might hide in a battle. The Philippians would have understood this, as their town was constantly guarded by an outpost of Roman soldiers, stationed there to shield their town. When we speak to God about all our concerns with thanksgiving, Paul said God sends his peace to safeguard our hearts and minds like the soldiers guarding Philippi.

But Paul gave them a second piece of guidance. He knew that freedom from worry did not come by trying to empty their minds of our concerns. Instead, once they'd given their worries to the Lord, they needed to fill their minds with other things. Paul gave these dear brothers and sisters and therefore us an entire list of worthy subjects, healthy material for meditation. Implied in this command is the fact that God cares what we think about and that we have the ability to control our thoughts. This is not any easy fix; our minds are sinful and lazy, prone to wandering and idolatry. But our brains can be trained to meditate on things that are true, innocent, honorable, and pleasing to God.

Paul described the stockpile of thoughts Christians can have on hand. These thoughts should be

- true—in the shape of the gospel with nothing false in them

- honorable—above reproach, things that others would respect

- right—to the Roman, this meant conforming to customs and laws of the land; to the Christian, it meant righteousness and conformity to God's law

- pure—something set apart and untouched by evil

- lovely—considered lovely by the world, like a Brahms string quartet or the work of a food pantry in a poor neighborhood

- admirable—positive in attitude as opposed to grumbling

- excellent—meaning morally excellent, something that contributes to the welfare of society

- praiseworthy—things that will earn God's commendation

What are some concrete examples of these? Things like the truth of the Trinity or the beauty of the fall colors. The giggle of a baby or a fellow saint's life story. A good soup recipe or proper technique for fly fishing. All of these are worthy of our attention and reflection, if kept in proper perspective and in submission to God. Paul concluded this instruction by pointing to himself as an example, not out of arrogance, but because he knew we needed skin-on representations of the cruciform life. He knew our eyes needed to see what a life shaped by the cross looked like. Paul's third encouragement is the most powerful. In our fight to train our minds against worry, selfishness, and a host of other destructive thought patterns, not only will God give us his peace, but the God of peace himself will be with us in our struggle.

Reflection Questions

4. Is it surprising to you to learn that much of this letter was to address a conflict between two women that played a powerful role in this church? When have you seen conflict between two key members in your church? What do you wish you could tell them from what you have learned from Philippians?

5. When Paul called them to rejoice, he was not referring to an emotion but rather to a point of view about their circumstances. "To rejoice in the Lord means that despite what we see around us, we can choose to let what God says be the most influential truth in our lives." What currently in your life would benefit from rejoicing over it?

6. When you feel anxious, what feels hard about coming to God in prayer?

7. Paul said God does three things when we take our worries to him instead of just ruminating on them in our own head: he gives us his peace, he fills our minds with helpful thoughts, and he gives us his presence. Which one of these do you most crave when you are anxious? Why?

8. Paul encouraged the Philippian believers after they had brought their burdens to the Lord to then fill their mind with worthy things to meditate on. Which of the eight things that he suggests would you like to spend more time meditating on?

Focus verse

Do not be anxious about anything, but in everything by prayer and supplication with thanksgiving let your requests be made known to God. And the peace of God, which surpasses all understanding, will guard your hearts and your minds in Christ Jesus.

Philippians 4:6–7

Reflections, curiosities, frustrations:

Through Him Who Strengthens Me

Read Philippians 4:10–23

Observation Questions

1. In verse 10, what was Paul rejoicing in learning?

2. What did Paul say in verses 11–13 he had learned ?

3. What had the Philippians done for Paul financially?

Interpretation

Philippians 4:10–13. Apparently Paul had not received any gifts from the Philippian church for quite some time. They sent him money multiple times in the past, and then came a long silence. Paul recognized that this church hadn't had the opportunity to give him any financial help. It's likely that Paul had been moving around the Roman prison system and had been hard to track. Word of mouth and hand delivered-letters took time.

In the meantime, God was continuing to teach Paul how to live above his circumstances. Notice that Paul had "learned" to be content. This implies that he, and we, are not born with this ability. Our hearts want more, different, better. We long for comfort and ease. We are easily controlled by our circumstances and surroundings. Contentment seems like a pipe dream—unattainable. But Paul continually used himself as an example for the Philippian Christians, someone to be imitated. And so, as impossible as it may seem, he shared with us his secret. First, he wrote that learning contentment is not magical or free of pain. It is a process that involves living through the very ups and downs we want so badly to avoid. Paul lived through humiliation and abundance. He went to bed hungry and knew days of plenty. Here is Paul's secret, and a verse that is so often taken terribly out of context: "I can do all things through him who strengthens me."

The "all things" here is not any outlandish endeavor we dream up but is the stuff of verse 12. Paul can be content in any circumstance, whether hungry and cold or full and warm, because of, and only because of, Jesus's power. He doesn't do this by looking inward, by amazing self-restraint or self-discipline. The secret he had learned is that of dependence. He leaned on, abided in, begged of, delighted in, and looked to Jesus. In everything. Not only did he do this when he was in need—in humble, hard circumstances—but also when he had plenty. The danger of self-sufficiency in times of plenty is just as menacing as the struggle to be content in times of drought. In these two extremes and all the places in between, Paul points us toward constant dependence on Christ.

Philippians 4:14–18. Any kind of partnership with Paul was potentially dangerous. He acknowledged the Philippians' longtime partnership with him in his mission, calling it in the Greek "fellowshipping with me in my suffering." It was not just the money that was helpful to Paul but the encouragement it brought with it. Notice, though, that Paul was more excited about what the gift they sent him meant for their spiritual lives. Paul knew that a fairly poor church pooling together a sum of money and sending it with a brother on an expensive journey didn't just come out of nowhere. It meant rich things were happening in the church spiritually. It meant God was growing the kingdom in their hearts. This is what excited Paul so much about the gift they had sent.

In their day, it would have been proper for Paul to repay their gift by sending a gift of his own. Clearly, he was unable to reciprocate. Instead, Paul reframed their contribution as a gift given to God by pulling on Old Testament sacrificial imagery (Leviticus 1:9). Once the bull had been prepared, cut, washed, and so on, parts of it were burned on the altar of God. The aroma pleased God, not because he had a penchant for steak, but because of the obedience and willingness of the one sacrificing. Paul equated the giving of this little church to that sort of sacrifice.

It pleased God and was evidence of fruit in their lives. In the same way, we can please God with our actions. We broken, sinful, selfish people can somehow bring pleasure to the God of the universe with our lives. This is a thrilling and unbelievable thought.

Philippians 4:19–23. Surely people in the community gave up specific things in order to send money to Paul. Paul assured them that God was aware of this and would indeed give them their daily bread. His words bring to mind Matthew 6, where Jesus speaks about the clothes, food, and drink we all need. Paul assured these dear ones that just as they had sought first the kingdom of God and his righteousness, so God would supply their daily needs.

Paul closed his letter with all of the affection that opened it. He added one last bit of encouragement, letting them know that even the household of Caesar was not safe from being infiltrated with the gospel of Christ. The very seat of power that sought to oppress them was slowly being permeated by the news that couldn't be contained. From the first paragraph of this letter to the last, Paul encouraged these Christians, his partners and collaborators, that God was at work. God is at work using our hardships. God is at work giving us examples to imitate. God is at work changing and sanctifying us. Be encouraged and rejoice, dear ones, for the Lord of glory, who willingly left all privilege behind and entered the darkness of suffering for you, is still at work.

Reflection Questions

4. Paul said that not receiving financial gifts from the Philippians for a while was hard but that God used it to teach his heart about contentment. When have you had a season of lack that did that for you?

5. Paul described the secret of contentment as growing in dependence on Jesus in all things, in times of plenty and in times of want. How does it differ from your view of contentment? What does dependence on Jesus look like practically for you?

6. Paul described the Philippians' financial contribution to him as a missionary as a way for them to share in his sufferings. Is this how you view supporting missionaries? How does this inform your heart more on that topic?

7. Paul said God would take care of the Philippians' needs as they took care of Paul's. Where are you currently serving or pouring out but concerned God won't provide for your needs? What do you need to repent of?

8. What are your takeaways from this study on the book of Philippians?

Focus verse

I know how to be brought low, and I know how to abound. In any and every circumstance, I have learned the secret of facing plenty and hunger, abundance and need. I can do all things through him who strengthens me.

Philippians 4:12–13

Reflections, curiosities, frustrations:

Acknowledgments

Hope: I have to thank all the people in my world who are always cheering me on. Dr. Ray-Ray, who equal parts makes me laugh and challenges me in all the places I get stuck, you are the best husband I could ask for. To my children, Cana, Thea, and Nias, who are so proud that their mom "has a book,' I love you on good days and bad. To my parents, who always have my back with love and words of belief in me. TCU Sisters, you are the ultimate hand holders who always cheer me on and love me every step of the way. To Joy and Natalie, your faith in me always surprises me and gives me courage when I need it the most! And to Renae, the best editor a girl could ask for, who polishes us up while always telling us this is good stuff and worthy to be written.

Chris: To my coffee fairy, you know who you are. You have literally made my thoughts more clear on many a day, and I am thankful for your tangible help. To Michael, who, whether he likes it or not, has become my first line of defense for all theological questions; you are still my favorite human. To Rebecca Brown, you have met me in the darkest places and not been ashamed of me. You help me keep going. RT and Jen, your voices on my Vox are often a lifeline. To the S-moms, thank you for being my constant encouragement and for making me laugh. Mollie, I still can't believe I get to live in the same town with you. You are such a safe place. Ally, you've opened our eyes to a whole new world of how God loves us, and that knowledge has made its way into my writing. And Renae, you work magic, practical magic.

Notes

Study 1. To All the Saints: Philippians 1:1–11

1. Karl Barth, qtd. in Garland, "Philippians," 189.

2. Fee, *Paul's Letter to the Philippians*, 70.

Study 2. Christ Is Proclaimed: Philippians 1:12–18

1. Fee, *Paul's Letter to the Philippians*, 110–11.

2. Garland, "Philippians," 199.

Study 3. Sharing in Christ's Suffering: Philippians 1:19–30

1. Fee, *Paul's Letter to the Philippians*, 162.

2. Silva, *Philippians*, 83.

Study 4: The Name Above Every Name: Philippians 2:1–11

1. Garland, "Philippians," 215.

Study 5. God Works in You: Philippians 2:12–18

1. Fee, *Paul's Letter to the Philippians,* 257.

Study 6. Fellow Workers: Philippians 2:19–30

1. Chapman, *Philippians,* 172.

2. Garland, "Philippians," 240.

Study 7. The Surpassing Worth of Knowing Christ: Philippians 3:1–11

1. Chapman, *Philippians,* 198.

2. Silva, *Philippians,* 157.

3. Fee, *Paul's Letter to the Philippians,* 320.

Study 8. We Await a Savior: Philippians 3:12–21

1. Garland, "Philippians," 171.

2. Ferguson, *Let's Study Philippians,* 90.

Study 9. Rejoice in the Lord Always: Philippians 4:1–9

1. Ferguson, *Let's Study Philippians,* 99.

Works Cited

Chapman, David. *Philippians: Rejoicing and Thanksgiving.* Focus on the Bible. Scotland, UK: Christian Focus, 2012.

Fee, Gordon. *Paul's Letter to the Philippians.* Grand Rapids, MI: William B. Eerdmans, 1995.

Ferguson, Sinclair B. *Let's Study Philippians.* Carlisle, PA: The Banner of Truth Trust, 1997.

Garland, David E. "Philippians." In *Ephesians–Philemon.* Vol. 12 of *The Expositor's Bible Commentary,* rev. ed., edited by Tremper Longman III and David E. Garland. Grand Rapids, MI: Zondervan, 2006.

Silva, Moisés. *Philippians,* 2nd ed. Baker Exegetical Commentary on the New Testament. Grand Rapids, MI: Baker Academic, 2005.

The Story of At His Feet Studies

A few years ago, Hope started looking for materials for the women's fall Bible study at our church. While she found a great number of quality Bible studies, she had a hard time finding studies written for women by women who were reformed. She also had a tough time finding in-depth studies of the Scripture that didn't take a whole lot of time. In a moment of desperation, Hope asked Chris if she would be willing to co-write a study on Romans, convincing her by asking, "I mean, really, how hard could it be?" And so it began. Weekly emails back and forth, Chris deep in commentaries, Hope mulling over questions, tweaking, editing, asking, pondering. A group of women at Redeemer Presbyterian Church in Lincoln, Nebraska, patiently bore with us as we experimented with them every week and learned to find our rhythm as writers.

Two years later, Hope approached Chris again, softening her up by telling her she could choose any book she wanted: 1 Samuel it was. Old Testament narrative is the best. Another study was born. About this time, women started asking us for copies of the two studies we had written. While trying to send endless PDFs to people around the country via email, a pastor friend who happens to be a publisher approached Chris and Hope at a party, offering to publish the Bible studies. Suddenly, we had a way to get these into the hands of women who could use them. This had been the point of the whole enterprise—to help make the book of Romans accessible to women. But what would the name be?

During the first century, when Jesus walked the earth, a Jewish rabbi would have been surrounded by his students, with some of the men sitting at his feet to learn and listen. This was the custom, the understood norm of the day. But in Luke 10:39, *Mary* sat at the feet of Jesus. Mary, a woman, was taught by this unconventional rabbi. Mary was given the dignity of taking in his words, his pauses, his tone. To Jesus, she was every bit as worthy of his teaching as the men in the room were—and so are we, his women students today. And so we are At His Feet Bible Studies, hoping to sit at the feet of Jesus while we study his Word.

Other At His Feet Studies

We pray that you will continue to sit at the feet of Jesus, studying his Word. To help you with this, we have also written these Bible studies:

1 Samuel (16 studies)
Psalms (13 studies)
Lamentations (7 studies)
Luke: Part 1 (13 studies)
Luke: Part 2 (14 studies)
Luke: Part 3 (12 studies)
The Servant King: A Study of the Gospel of Luke (10 studies)
El rey siervo: Un estudio sobre el evangelio de Lucas (en español, 10 estudios)
Romans, 2nd ed. (10 studies)
Galatians (8 studies)
Gálatas (en español, 8 estudios)
Colossians (10 studies)

You can find all of our studies at athisfeetstudies.com.

www.ingramcontent.com/pod-product-compliance
Lightning Source LLC
Chambersburg PA
CBHW081721120626
46550CB00010B/3195